Growing Through Arts!™

by *Aleksandra* ^{SM}

Twist
A MUSICAL

BY *Aleksandra* ®

MUSIC SERIES
BOOK 3

Illustrations by Elizaveta Efimova

Special Thanks to Russian Pointe Dance Boutique, Nikolas Wenzel, Auditorium Theatre of Roosevelt University, and Rudolf Steiner School of Ann Arbor

Library of Congress Control Number: 2011934342
ISBN 978-0-9838325-2-2

Production Date: December 20, 2011
Printing Plant Location: Everbest Printing Co. Ltd.,
    Nansha, China
Job/Batch #: EPC-RN-103612.1

FROM *Aleksandra* ®

The magic of an opera, the breathtaking sweep of a symphony, the rousing spirit of a musical . . .

Welcome to the Music Series from **Growing Through Arts**®!

One of the greatest treasures in human life is music. The impact of music on *children's* lives is especially powerful. Far beyond providing simple entertainment, music lays a foundation for success in academics, career, relationships, and life itself. Participation in the musical arts helps children develop critical skills such as spatial reasoning, fine motor movement, and language processing. At the same time, it builds vital character traits such as focus, discipline, confidence, creativity, respect for a teacher, and the ability to work independently and in a group.

It gives me special pleasure to share with you the timeless stories of Snow Maiden (Opera), Peter and the Wolf (Symphony), and Oliver Twist (Musical). In these delightful tales your child will be transported into the magical world of musical performance. Each story introduces new musical terms and performance concepts, but the learning doesn't stop there. Through uplifting storylines, the books also teach important life values, such as the need for courage and compassion; the rewards of hard work; the beauty of unconditional love; the value of overcoming fears; and the gifts of following your passions.

It is my deepest wish that these books provide countless hours of education, discovery, time-sharing, and meaningful conversation for you and your child. I hope in some tiny way they inspire your child to greater achievement and fulfillment, and empower him or her to be a better global citizen.

Thank you for making **Growing Through Arts**® a part of your lives!

Ever Growing Through Arts,
Aleksandra
www.aleksandra.com

How to Use This Book.

- Read the story to your child many times to encourage memory and to explore the themes more deeply.

- Pretend you are in a theatre, listening and watching the "musical performance" unfold on stage!

- Read and discuss **Miss Aleksandra's Themes & Values**, integrated throughout the book, and look for ways to relate them to your child's life.

- Look for **bold words** in the story and look up their meanings in **Miss Aleksandra's Glossary**. Help your child learn about music and the performing arts.

- Create "teachable moments" with your child by learning letter- and music-themed words in the **Music Alphabet by Aleksandra** (sold separately), which integrates characters, concepts and story elements from the storybook.

- **Stage Scene Play Sets** (sold separately) bring characters to life!

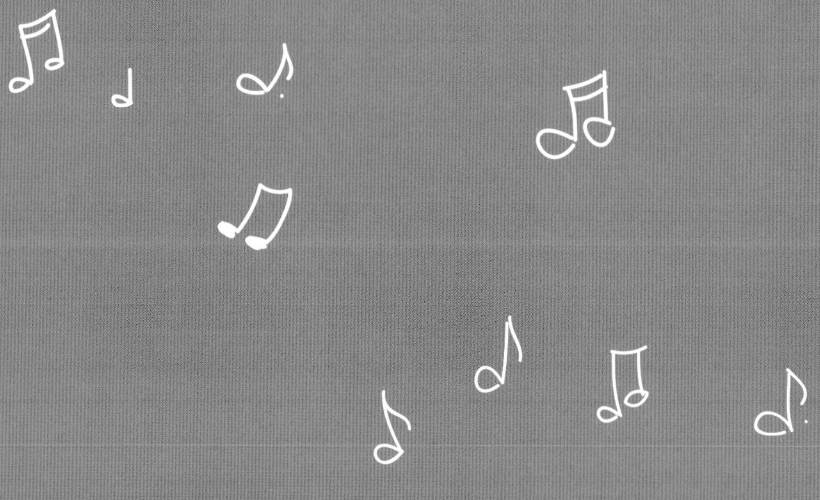

All day long, Ozzie was so excited he could hardly do his schoolwork. Tonight was the **premiere** of a new **musical** of *Oliver Twist.* And Ozzie was in it! He was part of the show's **ensemble**. That meant he sang in the group **numbers**, but didn't have any **solos**.

Oliver Twist *is a wonderful book by Charles Dickens that has inspired more than one musical. You might want to read it someday!*

Ozzie had a beautiful voice, but he was shy about it because sometimes the other boys made fun of him. So he didn't tell anyone at school about the show.

Is it nice to make fun of others? Have you ever kept something secret because you didn't want anyone to make fun of you?

MISS Aleksandra's®
THEMES & VALUES

After dinner, it was time for Ozzie to go to the theater. "I love you!" said his foster mom. "Break a leg!" That's a funny way people say "good luck" to **actors**. It doesn't mean *really* break a leg.

Backstage, the performers were buzzing with excitement.

Then the **director**, Ms. Karl, announced, "Everyone, please gather **center stage**! I have some terrible news."

When the whole **cast** was together, Ms. Karl said, "I'm afraid Brendan really *broke* his leg and won't be able to perform."

Everyone gasped! Brendan had the **lead role** of Oliver! How could they do the show without him?

🍃 *It's polite to say "please" whenever you ask anyone to do something. Do you say "please" when you ask for things?*

"Luckily," said Ms. Karl, "We have a very talented **understudy**—Ozzie!"

It was true. Ozzie *was* the understudy. That meant he had practiced the role of Oliver in case Brendan ever got sick.

It's smart to prepare in case something goes wrong, don't you think?

He knew all the **blocking**, the **lines**, and the songs. But he never thought he'd really have to *perform* as Oliver!

"No!" shouted Ozzie. "I can't!"

He ran and hid in the **dressing room**.

After a while he heard Ms. Karl's voice. "Ozzie, I know you're scared," she said, "but if you don't perform tonight, you'll let a lot of people down—the audience, the other actors, and, most of all, yourself."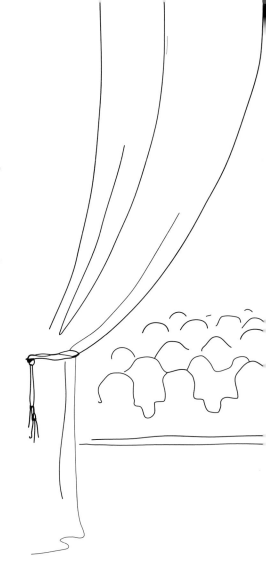

Ozzie thought about this. He didn't want to let anyone down, but he *really* didn't want to play the big role of Oliver. He didn't know what to do!

"Do you trust me?" asked Ms. Karl. Ozzie said he did. "Then I'm going to help you get through this show. Okay?"

Ozzie didn't answer.

"Think about the character of Oliver," Ms. Karl said. "You and he are alike in many ways. I think that can help you perform the role!"

There's a saying in theater, "The show must go on!" What do you think that means? Do you think it's important?

Ozzie promised to play Brendan's role in case anything ever went wrong. Do you think people should keep their promises?

9

Ozzie thought about it. In the famous story, the character Oliver loses his parents as a baby and grows up in strange places where he doesn't feel he belongs.

Ozzie had lost *his* parents, too! He had lived in three different foster homes before now.

His new foster parents said they loved him and wanted to adopt him, but sometimes he wondered if he really belonged with them.

I think your real family is the people who love you, even if they're not the same people you were born with. What do you think?

11

Ozzie thought some more. In the story, other children made fun of Oliver and tried to make him do things he didn't want to do.

Ozzie knew what that felt like, too. "I'll do the part, Ms. Karl," he said quietly. "I mean, I'll *try*."

"That's wonderful, Ozzie. Just try your best. Now hurry and get into costume!"

It's important to always try your best. When was a time you did your best?

12

"**Places!**" shouted the **stage manager**.

The curtain rose!

The show began with a famous scene where Oliver and some other children were living in a cold, dreary workhouse. They worked hard all day but were never given enough to eat.

As Ozzie waited to go on stage, Ms. Karl could see him shaking. She knelt beside him and whispered, "In the first song, Oliver speaks up and asks his mean boss for more food for him and the other children. This is a scary thing for Oliver to do. Have you ever been scared to open your mouth, Ozzie?"

"Yes! I'm scared right now!" said Ozzie.

"Good," said Ms. Karl. "Then put that feeling into the song!"

Have you ever felt afraid to speak up? Did you feel better after you did it?

Suddenly, Ozzie knew how to sing the first song. All he had to do was use his *real feelings*. He stepped on stage. He was still shaking, but that was okay because his *character*, Oliver, was supposed to be scared, too. He sang the first **verse**:

Please, sir, I don't mean to intrude
Please, sir, I don't mean to be rude
But me and my mates need
to have some more food

As Ozzie sang, his own fear made the song feel real to him. To the audience, too! And then, as the *character* Oliver grew more confident, so did Ozzie! After the song, there was loud applause.
Ozzie **exited** the stage.

"You just learned an important lesson about performing," Ms. Karl whispered. "When you put *real feelings* into it, it comes alive!"  Ozzie felt better now. He couldn't wait for the next number!

"For the rest of the show," said Ms. Karl, "you're going to use real feelings about *your* life to bring *Oliver's* feelings to life. Okay, Ozzie?" Ozzie nodded.

And so that's what he did. When the *character* Oliver ran away to a strange new place called London, Ozzie thought of the nervous way *he* felt each time he started in a strange new school.

Feelings *are the most important part of any performance—acting, singing, or dancing. When the performer's feelings are real, the audience feels it too.*

Did you ever feel scared when you had to go to a new place? When was that?

16

When thieves tried to make the *character* Oliver do bad things, Ozzie thought about the mixed-up way *he* felt one time when some boys at school told him to take a book that didn't belong to him.

When the *character* Oliver was taken in by a kind man named Mr. Brownlow, Ozzie thought about how happy *he* was to find his foster parents . . . and how worried he was that he might lose them.

MISS *Aleksandra's*® THEMES & VALUES

Did anyone ever ask you to do something that seemed wrong to you? How did that make you feel?

"You're doing a fantastic job!" Ms. Karl told him during intermission. Ozzie's face lit up. But then he remembered that his hardest solo was coming up. It was the show's **finale**, a song called "I Know Who I Am."

"I can't sing that one, Ms. Karl," he said, feeling a heavy weight in his chest. "I've never gotten it right, even in **rehearsal**!"

"Think about that song, Ozzie," Ms. Karl said. "When Oliver sings it, he's just found out who his real mother was, and he's proudly telling the whole world who *he* is. Do *you* ever want to tell the whole world who you are?"

"Yes," replied Ozzie, "I want to say, 'I'm a singer and an actor!' I don't want to hide it anymore."

"Well then, I'm going to tell you a little secret, Ozzie. From the moment you **auditioned**, I wanted to give you the lead role. I could see how talented you were, but I knew you didn't believe it. Now I think you do. So go sing that song, and tell the whole world who you are!"

Is there something you'd like to tell the whole world about you?
Ozzie has talent, he just doesn't have confidence yet. Do you think it's good to have both? What are you talented at? Do you have confidence?

As the **accompaniment** for the final song began, Ozzie wanted to run away, but then he thought about the real feelings he wanted to express. He forgot his fear, opened his mouth, and . . .

. . . Before he knew it, he was singing the final lyrics,

"I Know Who I Am! I Know Who I Am!" and the audience was jumping to its feet, cheering wildly.

When you love what you're doing, your fears and worries seem to disappear. What's something that you love to do? It feels good to be known for who you truly are!

20

Ozzie looked out at the seats and saw his foster parents
clapping harder than anyone and shouting,

"We love you, Ozzie!
We love you!"

And just like his character, Oliver,
Ozzie knew he had found his home.

Maybe Ozzie has found his
home in more than one way.
What do you think?

The next day, the **critics** gave the show a **rave review**. They all said how wonderful Ozzie's performance was.

Their words were nice, but Ozzie didn't need to read them. Because now he believed them himself.

When you believe in yourself, what other people think isn't so important! Do you believe in yourself?

Glossary

actors

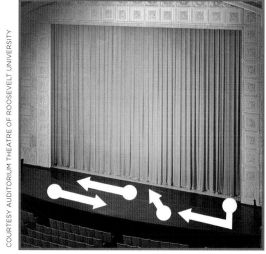

blocking

Accompaniment is music that plays while a singer (or group of singers) sings a melody.

Performers in a play or musical are called **actors**. Actors pretend to be characters on stage.

When singers and actors **audition**, they try out for a role and hope they get picked.

Blocking is the movements and positions of actors on stage.

The whole group of actors in a show is called the **cast**.

Center stage means the middle area of the stage. Up stage, down stage, stage right, and stage left are terms used to describe other areas of the stage.

A theater **critic** attends a performance and then writes or talks about it for others.

The **director** is the person in charge of a play or musical. The director decides how the play will be performed and helps the actors to understand their roles.

Performers use a **dressing room** to put on makeup and costumes.

cast

dressing room

ensemble

lead role

An **ensemble** is a group of singers or actors that perform together on stage.

To **exit** means to go offstage.

The **finale** is the last song in a musical. It is usually an important *number* (see below).

The **lead role** is the main character in a play, musical, or opera.

The words that actors speak in a play are called their **lines**.

A **musical** is a kind of show that has both songs and spoken lines. It's different from an opera in which all of the lines are sung.

A **number** is another word for a song in a show.

When the word "**Places**!" is called, actors need to get in position for the show to start.

A **premiere** is the first performance of a show by a company.

A **rave review** means that a critic (see above) really loved a show.

Rehearsal is the period of time when performers learn and practice their parts.

solo

A **solo** is a song a performer sings alone.

It's the job of the **stage manager** to make sure everything runs smoothly during a performance.

An **understudy** learns the role of another actor in case that actor ever needs to be replaced.

A **verse** is the part of a song before the chorus. The chorus is the "main" part of the song and it is often repeated more than once.

Make Every Moment a Teachable Moment!

GROWING THROUGH ARTS® COLLECTION

BALLET SERIES

The Nutcracker Ballet by Aleksandra®

The Cinderella Ballet by Aleksandra®

The Sleeping Beauty Ballet by Aleksandra®

The Nutcracker Ballet Practice & Play Book by Aleksandra®

The Cinderella Ballet Practice & Play Book by Aleksandra®

The Sleeping Beauty Ballet Practice & Play Book by Aleksandra®

MUSIC SERIES

The Snow Maiden Opera by Aleksandra®

The Peter and the Wolf Symphony by Aleksandra®

Twist, A Musical by Aleksandra®

INTERACTIVE LEARNING TOYS AND ACCESSORIES

For each beautifully illustrated storybook in the Ballet and Music Series, we offer several interactive learning companion pieces including Practice & Play Books, Stage Scene Play Sets, an Alphabet Set and dress-up accessories such as ballet slippers, tiaras, tutus, leotards and tights to bring the characters in the storybooks to life.

WWW.GROWINGTHROUGHARTS.COM

Aleksandra Efimova is the founder of **Growing Through Arts**®
and President of Russian Pointe, a brand of luxury ballet shoes
specially handcrafted and imported directly from Russia. Russian
Pointe's flagship Russian Pointe Dance Boutique on Chicago's
Magnificent Mile features the most sought-after pointe shoes and
dancewear accessories as well as the entire Growing Through
Arts Collection. Born in St. Petersburg, Russia, Aleksandra
graduated from the renowned Art School at the Hermitage
State Art Museum and received training in classical dance,
art and academics. In 1993, she moved to the United States
where she started her first successful company while still
an undergraduate student. An Alumna of the prestigious
Harvard Business School, she has dedicated herself
to sharing access to and enjoyment of the arts,
and to building bridges among people of
different cultures. Her passion for the arts,
Russian culture and international relations has
helped propel Aleksandra Enterprises into
the international spotlight as a company that
transcends boundaries of language and culture.
To learn more visit: **www.aleksandra.com**.

rough Ar Grou

Growing Thro